Routine Bloodwork

Finalist for the Charlotte Mew Prize

Routine Bloodwork

Colleen McKee

HEADMISTRESS PRESS

Copyright © 2020 by Colleen McKee
All rights reserved.

ISBN 9781733534543

This book may not be reproduced, in whole or in part, including illustrations, in any form (beyond that permitted by Sections 107 and 108 of the U.S. Copyright Law and except by reviewers for the public press), without written permission from the publishers.

Cover art © 2007 by Jemma Watts. Fish 1. www.jemmajwatts.com
Cover & book design by Mary Meriam.

PUBLISHER
Headmistress Press
60 Shipview Lane
Sequim, WA 98382
Telephone: 917-428-8312
Email: headmistresspress@gmail.com
Website: headmistresspress.blogspot.com

Dedicated to Ratfag

Contents

In Her Famous Fur-Lined Skirt	1
Drunken Alphabet	3
Lift Up Your Tongue and Say Ahh	4
I Love You Enough	5
The Drunk Punk on the Funhouse Pinball Machine	6
The Care and Nourishment of Lies	8
Maximum Setting	9
Routine Bloodwork	10
The Corkscrew	15
Terminals and Gates	16
Gingkos	17
The Wayside Inn	18
The Window on Wyoming Street	23
The Pigeon	24
The Fly	25
Despite Your Death	26
Meditation on the 58 Bus	27
Some Mornings	28
Fickle Flowered Boughs	29
Just Before the Wedding I Did Not Want to Attend	31
Humans Suck (or, The Gospel of Ratfag)	33
Notes on the Poems	37
Acknowledgements	39
About the Author	41

In Her Famous Fur-Lined Skirt

> *Every girl ought to walk a tightrope. It develops a rare set of muscles and teaches one how to walk properly on the street.*
> —Internationally acclaimed aerialist Bird Millman, in a 1913 interview with the Milwaukee News

But why would a girl want to walk
on the street, properly
or otherwise,
when she could promenade
across the sky?

In a pink velvet dress
twirling a crimson parasol,
Bird hops on the sides
of her ballet flats
along a string
between skyscrapers.
The brash Chicago wind
throws itself at her,
licks her hair
like a rowdy puppy.

Most women were hung up on clotheslines
as Miss Millman explored
the umbilical cord
joining
heaven
and earth.

She went through three husbands
before she was fifty. Did men
love her best from afar?—
The gasps, the terrified smiles
were mirrors flashing the sun,

magnifying its radiance, as the wind
flirted with her skirt
and she lifted
her legs and lowered
her fanny laughing
at death
and earthbound
fools.

Drunken Alphabet

A is for absinthe,
B is for button
open at her collar,
D is for dirty,
extra-dirty martinis
for this girl,
her icy jonquil kisses
love-me-not lips
open, parting, queer,
revealing some thing?
(or nothing)…ululations
of pretty
vacant words,
x-rated promises
you know might mean nothing, but
you play with the
zippers of her motorcycle jacket
and buy her another drink:

A is for Absolut,
B is for gorgeous blur…

Lift Up Your Tongue and Say Ahh

Her mind's a thermometer dropped on the floor—no way to measure
pyretic desires—metallic drops scatter under the door,
the bed, they nest in electrical wires…quicksilver shimmy
and shimmer galore, sputtering grasping greased vanity,
brittle sweet romances, manic dolor—she plays hide and seek
with her own sanity. *Where are my gloves? What is the time?*
Where do you run to, coldsweating dream? Why do I crawl
without reason or rhyme? Self-splitting toxin, see how it gleams.
Mercury silver, Mercury gray: a god whose chief talent
is flying away.

I Love You Enough

I love you enough to ask you
when was the last time you washed this carpet
and why won't you take off your boots
when I mop?
I love you enough to place

your photo on the Fridgidaire.
I love you enough to wear
your band of braided silver.
I love you enough to ask you
who is that woman

at my kitchen table
nibbling at the muffins
I made for you this morning,
that woman you were with
so very late last night?

I see the way the red
comes to your cheeks and your neck
whenever she laughs and I love you
enough to tell you,
it's time for her to go.

The Drunk Punk on the Funhouse Pinball Machine

Fire-red globes revolve and lick and light the silver ball
that flirts and hides, zags and zigs, slips
and is lost in epileptic lights,
the cackling machine's staticky squeals.
"Sugar, don't do me like that!"
(Agony tastes like Marlboro Reds,
her beery cottonmouth tongue…)
"Where's the ball? Where's the ball?" By the creepy babydoll!
It's screwed into the board, it twitches and leers, a crack up its cheek—
At a well-timed slap of a button—"Yes!
Yes! A perfect yes!" her ball
bangs off a flipper
painted with a dancing girl,
her skirt up to her ears—now
a mechanical trunk, suddenly part of the game, twists open,
sinking her prize but promising more, and
bonus balls pour down like biblical hail!
"What the fuck?" She flails at controls like a sweaty schmuck
while fallen balls rattle and skip
round the grumbling bowels of the game,
a cacophony that only reminds her
of her mean, cute, crazy ex, words
that rebound round her skull,
ricochet cross her heart,
sputter inside her stomach.
The sounds clatter down her spine,
she thrusts her hips, she yanks,
hope against hope, to get leverage,
to manipulate the path of that mercurial sphere…
See her shake the machine
as though she didn't know
gravity was always against her.
And as the last ball's swallowed whole,
all sound sucked under,

a quicksilver world down the drain,
the game's neon nerves
collapsed in shadow—the circus
fled—"No!
No! You son of a...
No!" She sweats and stammers, kicks
the machine, and digs
in her pockets again.

The Care and Nourishment of Lies

Water them too little and they dry out.
Then spores fills the air, coughing,
sneezing, like soft splinters up your nose.

Water lies too much, their stems
snake and snap, carnivorous
plants that nibble and rasp
at nails, grasp at toes.

Lies require darkness,
but not enough light,
and lies die of vanity.

Don't forget to fertilize.
Stop your ears
with shit.

Maximum Setting

My affections tumble fast
in the amped-up, defective
dryer of my mind, sparking
with static electricity,
mucked up and balled
with gray lint of doubt.

Gas-blasting machine,
mad-headed machinations,
energy most inefficient,
snap-banging, zipper-slapping drum
of desire, churning and chewing
buttons and matches, groaning and clanging,
splitting seams, spitting quarters,
whirring and whirling, rapid-cycle lover,
melting lipstick and making confetti
of ink-stained cocktail napkins!

All-night machine,
in your hot mouth, nothing
ever gets clean.

Routine Bloodwork

On February 10th, the *Post-Dispatch*
reported that a broken heart
actually can kill.

Scientists have finally verified
what poets have claimed for centuries.
But in this poet's shotgun apartment,

there will be little rejoicing,
though the note you slipped under my door
at dawn (when you knew I was up)

has not quite riven my heart. No,
each muscular ventricle
continues to predictably pump, and I venture out

into the factual world, shoe leather
slapping the sidewalk,
silk and rayon

swaying round my hips,
lingerie now worn for warmth.
I observe the familiar urban ecology,

listing reasons to live
on the loyal, gray paper of my brain:
the quiet sparkle of glass in cement, the vermilion

bare stalks of bushes. I recall
that these are forsythia; they do not seem so
without blooms.

The train opens itself to me
with mechanical generosity, as it does
morning after morning,

and deposits me at the hospital
recently hit by a wrecking ball.

Half built up and half torn down, acres
of rusted, cracked iron beams,

torn insulation, dusty glass, tubes
that might have kept someone alive:

I walk up the stairs, roll up my sleeve. What
are a few more drops?

The Corkscrew

From your leopard-print bed on Division St.,
I walk 35 blocks back to Belmont,
where my sister's couch is home for 5 days.
My skin feels wonderfully filthy, soft,
salty from your spit and our sweat.
I'm brown as bread from the sun,
cottonmouthed from short swatches of sleep.
From dawn to noon you corkscrewed
your long freckled body
round my body as you slept,
your elbows and knees jutting everywhere,
and snoring in my ear—not a snore
but a purr. I wouldn't trade that
for sleep. Or anything.

At 30th and Morrison,
I hear the tuneless melody of
Lucky Larry's ice cream truck.
I stoop in my polka-dot sundress
to sniff yet another
ludicrously fat white rose
stained with scarlet lipstick.
How easy and impossible
it would be to stay,
avoid airports and rent.
To just let my feet
do what they want.
To feel human
instead of grown-up.

I don't understand the way this world works.
But I know I'll remember you,
your watchful green eyes, your huge hands
that listen and hold every part of me,
every part bruised and breathing,
every part blessed with salt.

Terminals and Gates

I love you in PDX, in OHD,
in STL, with K7
written on my thin wrist.
With a stomach full of sea
and the sound of a fire
on my headset—static
and a slow piano. With the carpet's
blue swirl like the pattern
of the ocean, & not like the ocean
at all. I love you with my family
2000 miles away. I love you with
my body an entire
state away. The crumpled
map of my dress. The lost
& found of my pen. The page
instead of a kiss. The scratch
of a bright red pen in place
of my nails on your back.
A song ends, then begins again.
I look up: a hall of blue & white
numbers as far as I can see. Soon
the gate will be open.

Gingkos

1.

We kissed in the grove, where gingkos shook
and slanted loose their leaves—
bruise-gold blessings, papery yet real,
catching in your curls, my lap,
whispering to your wrists, scratching so soft
the lines in our palms: this
is the currency of heaven.

2.

Stuff your pockets with schedules,
plane tickets, breast feathers, stones
from my city.

3.

Shut the leaf in a book.
Open me again.

The Wayside Inn

In a rented bed, two restless friends
trace lines in each other's palms.
They don't notice the moon descend,

nor do they watch Orion ascend,
his arrow pointed at Gemini's arms.
In the rented bed, the restless friends

grasp each other's familiar limbs
as though to protect them from harm.
They do not notice the moon descend.

Kay is surprised by her year after year, still depends
on the sugar salt taste of her sweat the way she used to rely on the psalms.
In the rented bed, these two friends

have learned to hear only one voice in the dark, to pretend
Joan's ring encircles only air, to be as numb
to its unyielding gold as to the silver moon's descent.

Everything that has been shall be again,
but at five comes the quiet cry of the alarm,
and the unrested friends in the rented bed
rise as the moon fades and descends.

The Window on Wyoming Street

I shut the window
and hear a staticky sound,
a fly, trapped, spinning,

hurling himself at
his own dark reflection, thudding
against a blue

mirage sky. There's a
lesson I'm not ready
to learn.

The Pigeon

My heart is a pigeon hiding in the eaves,
a diligent bird pecking hard rice from the road.
My heart is not a dove. There is nothing
peaceful about it. My heart is common,
aggressive. It struts and fights.
Feathers missing,
my heart has only
one golden eye.

Gray as a rain-soaked sidewalk.
Sudden flashes of iris iridescence.
Scarlet claws clutch at the curb.

The Fly

I wake from dreams of fickle women
to a fly skimming over my body.
I flail my arms and fall into sleep.

I dream I am saddled
with twenty children, all
in identical tiny red coats. This fly

is kissing the back
of my knee. I kick;
he cycles furiously around me,

half spirals, whirlwinds—why
won't he leave? The window's
been open for days, but each

day begins exactly the same—
with the whine of a puny war in my ear
I drift into dreams of mazes and sex,

cities without centers,
tests I can't pass,
and the fly bounces from hip

to hip, nibbling on my ear
and sucking on my hair,
and I swat: I'm not dead yet.

Despite Your Death

you came to my room
as the sky began to pearl, and the sun
to slide over the ice.

You were dapper in your dusty top hat,
your old pea coat, a dufflebag
slung over your shoulder.

I'd been expecting you, met you
at the door, felt the cold
torn wool of your sleeve.

Casually you pulled from your pocket
a jewel, a tear-shaped diamond, big
as your hand.

The gem changed to a lotus:
sharp emerald leaves,
amethyst closed tips of petals.

It was all of one piece, one jewel.
It had its own light.
You offered it to me.

"Where did you *get* this?" I said.

"Oh, I found it in the underworld."

Meditation on the 58 Bus

I allow myself to be seduced by G-d, though I suspect
he cannot be trusted. By seduced
I don't mean a swan, a lightning bolt
or a storm of coins, but the way
spring light sidles up to the white
of a tight girl's T-shirt, the liquid
gleam on the edge
of a dented aluminum can
clinking its windswept path down DeBaliviere,
the window cracked open, warmth in my hands
closed on my lap, as though
I have something to hold onto.

Some Mornings

Some mornings, even
a year after your death,
any landscape will remind me of you:
foxglove violet as lilacs,
foxglove white as jade,
this deck railing
that held your back,
this rusty white boat
you never even saw
coming queerly close
to shore.

Fickle Flowered Boughs

The dead have dreams too, you know.
        They do not know they are dreaming, just as you
do not know you're alive.

In this dream, I walk down Pine Street.
        Fickle flowered boughs shade the boulevard
from the green white streetlights.

Redbuds, shining bronze hearts so still,
        cut out of a nearly full moon.
Magnolia blossoms, tattered flags

battered by yesterday's rain.
        Pear petals fall silent as stars.
Because it is cold, I wear a red coat,

rough wool the color of azaleas.
        Because I am dead, I do not use the sidewalk.
I walk in the ivy that lines the street.

It curls round my ankles but cannot keep me.
        In death, I walk straight, as I could not
in life. I approach my apartment complex.

Behind stained glass, my friends are singing,
        smoking with beautiful fingers
on rusted-out fire escapes, smashing

their windows and flirting with me, pretending
        their hands are not bleeding
as they borrow my very last broom.

See me in my pleated dancing dress
        spread over the floor like a deck
of cards, a glass of vodka

and scarlet juice held high
        like a torch. That was my house-
warming party. The other me, that other woman,

she is still there, starring in her own silent movie,
        black straps falling from her shoulders
in glamorous self-degradation.

A new broom sweeps away old ghosts.
        I don't wonder who has stolen my key.
All I want now is for one real pear

to drop from a white-feathered sky.

Just Before the Wedding I Do Not Want to Attend

On the wide rolling grounds of a schoolhouse
bounded by ferns and wild bamboo,
I wear a feather in my hair
at the request of the bride.
My high heels sink into Oregon mud.
Over the crowd, the ocean purrs.
Two months after the death
of my old flame, ankles aching,
I endure well-wishers
who ask, When will *you* marry?

I smile and nod politely.
The creature in my chest
grows claws.

I wander away from the crowd,
away from the salmon and figs,
from the chuppah, its red ribbons
whipping the wind.
I elude the bride, sick over split ends,
and my dad, the wide-eyed groom, stout
in his suit, galoshing around.
My sisters do hair, they laugh,
they dance, they do
everything right.

I wander off to a swingset,
grip the cool, thick chains,
hold on to their rattle and weight.
And with my spike heel,
I scratch the name of my dead lover
in damp summer sand.

I bend into the wind,
kick off those heels
and begin to ascend.

On the upswing, I glimpse
the ocean, a flat blue stripe,
calm, past the pines.
Mountain jays bark at the sun.
I pump and my iris silk skirt
billows over my thighs,
sand grits between my teeth.

Then, a sudden weight on the swingset—
creaking, whooping—who is it below?
Three old women, loud wedding guests,
pointing their toes at the sun.
They smile up at me, they rise—
our rippling skirts are silken flags,
golden, emerald, alizarin crimson.

Corsages go flying
and sandals thudding
into the earth
we leave behind.

Humans Suck (or, the Gospel of Ratfag)

I see the words *forgive yourself*
stenciled 3 times on my street,
40th, on my way
to the train.

I tap them lightly with my cane each morning,
hit them heavy limping home at dusk.
forgive yourself flashes in the streetlights in the rain
reflected in the junction box
on the corner of Martin Luther King.

Someone's stenciled HUMANS SUCK
a few times on 40th—probably someone else—
HUMANS SUCK is smudged
glopped in what looks to be blistering tar
bubbled up from some Oakland hellmouth.

I like the two together:
forgive yourself because
you're human. Humans suck.

forgive yourself is faded,
HUMANS SUCK more steadfast
despite the angry smear.
But I see *forgive*
burnished on the sidewalk
faint as old nickels and pennies.
It shows up better in the rain.
I see the words I need at my feet.

2.

This isn't the first time. Nine years ago,
just before I left St. Louis,

someone wrote FO GIVE YO SELF
small, brushed green
on a gutter on South Grand
around the corner from where we lived.

First saw it one frigid dawn
on the way to the bus.
It was a few months
after my best friend killed himself.

All through the ice, the long thaw,
the brief spring,
FO GIVE YO SELF
multiplied, the words
bigger, blacker,
sprayed at eye level
on stolid brick buildings
along South Grand.

I still saw my sweetheart's sexy ghost
strutting down Grand in striped bellbottoms, smoking
and giving me the stink eye, sometimes
just sticking out his tongue.

One summer dusk, looming over the highway,
seven stories up and ten feet tall,
FO GIVE YO SELF
outlined in gold,
bold on a gutted warehouse,
a swaying thing of splinters,
more wind than wood,
teetering over the Mississippi River.
Who risked their lives to write it?

Every time I see these words,
small or monumental,
I do forgive myself,
if only for that moment,

and bless the ones
who needed
to write it
and did.

I can walk
these cracked and crumbling cities
knowing someone
is blessing us all,
every wretched one of us,
no matter what we've done
or failed to do.

Notes on the Poems

"The Care and Nourishment of Lies": Apologies to Jacqueline Winspear, who wrote a historical novel with the wonderful title *The Care and Management of Lies*.

"Humans Suck (Or, the Gospel of Ratfag)": According to the *Riverfront Times*, someone who goes by Ratfag, Redd Foxx, and Ed Boxx is responsible for writing FO GIVE YO SELF all over St. Louis. Obviously, this is not the St. Louis-born actor Redd Foxx (long live his name). Some of the graffiti says, "REDD FOXX SAYS FO GIVE YO SELF." Who Ratfag/Redd Foxx/Ed Boxx is, whether this person works alone or with other aerosol evangelicals of mercy, is a mystery. Equally mysterious are the stencilers of Oakland.

My lover and friend mentioned in the poem identified as a bi, trans, genderqueer, feminine person. When we met, Miko was 20 and preferred the pronouns zhe, zher, zherself. Miko was completely out of the closet for years but seemed to lose morale after being physically attacked a few times for being feminine. Miko couldn't afford the surgery to have a more curvaceous body and was dismayed that many friends didn't support this goal anyway. At 30, he was managing a bar that was a bit rough around the edges (though many of the workers and regulars were wonderful, open-minded people). But Miko told me then that he was no longer trans or queer and that he should be called "he." So I am using masculine pronouns in this poem to honor his wishes, but it is uncomfortable as I question whether using "he" honors who Miko really was or just honors the closet that failed to protect him. No pronouns seem right. It may be that Miko's story can never be made right. I believe that he never "successfully" wished away queerness nor femininity and that the closet was part of the reason he committed suicide in 2008.

"Just Before the Wedding I Did Not Want to Attend": A chuppah is a canopy made of long sticks with flowering branches and ribbons. In Jewish weddings, the couple is married under the chuppah.

"The Wayside Inn": "Everything that has been shall be again" is from an essay by William Butler Yeats.

Acknowledgements

Alt Beast: The Zine: "The Care and Nourishment of Lies"

The Sigh Press: "The Fly" and "The Pigeon"

Haight Ashbury Literary Journal: "Lift Up Your Tongue and Say Ahh"

Thanks

To teachers and fellow students in the workshops in the MFA in Creative Writing program at the University of Missouri-St. Louis for their suggestions on a few of these poems. I'm also grateful to friends in the following writers groups in St. Louis, San Francisco, and Berkeley: It's My Monkey!, The Sunday Morning Gospel Hour, The San Francisco Writers Workshop, and the Au Coquelet Writers Group (including that long migratory bird, Lee Foust). Friends, without all of your honest and generously given advice, this book would be a weaker book, and my life would be a sadder life.

About the Author

Colleen McKee is the author of four other collections of memoir, poetry, and fiction: *The Kingdom of Roly-Polys* (Pedestrian Poets Series, 2017); *Nine Kinds of Wrong* (JKPublishing, 2013); *A Partial List of Things I Have Done for Money* (JKPublishing, 2011); and *My Hot Little Tomato* (Cherry Pie Press Midwestern Women Poets Series, 2007). With Amanda Crowell Stiebel, she is co-editor of an anthology of personal narratives, *Are We Feeling Better Yet? Women Speak About Health Care in America* (PenUltimate, 2008). Colleen earned her MFA in Creative Writing from the University of Missouri-St. Louis.

Colleen comes from rural Missouri, the green, humid song of cicadas. Raised by hippie artists, leather queens, Pentecostals, and Russian Jews, she grew up speaking Yiddish, Yenglish, and English with a Southern accent. She lived for twenty years in South Saint Louis, which smells like fried chicken and hops. She now lives in Oakland, California, which smells like fried chicken and weed.

She usually likes her job as a teaching assistant in art and architecture classes in San Francisco. She is working on a novel about a possibly cursed circus; the novel is tentatively titled *Shlomo the Strong Man and the Uninvited Guests*. When she is not writing or teaching, she loves to sing in Yiddish and other languages with the band The Klezmerachis.

Find Colleen at ColleenMcKee.Blogspot.com, or contact her at colleenbethmckee@gmail.com

HEADMISTRESS PRESS BOOKS

Tender Age - Luiza Flynn-Goodlett
Low-water's Edge - Jean A. Kingsley
Routine Bloodwork - Colleen McKee
Queer Hagiographies - Audra Puchalski
Why I Never Finished My Dissertation - Laura Foley
The Princess of Pain - Carolyn Gage & Sudie Rakusin
Seed - Janice Gould
Riding with Anne Sexton - Jen Rouse
Spoiled Meat - Nicole Santalucia
Cake - Jen Rouse
The Salt and the Song - Virginia Petrucci
mad girl's crush tweet - summer jade leavitt
Saturn coming out of its Retrograde - Briana Roldan
i am this girl - gina marie bernard
Week/End - Sarah Duncan
My Girl's Green Jacket - Mary Meriam
Nuts in Nutland - Mary Meriam & Hannah Barrett
Lovely - Lesléa Newman
Teeth & Teeth - Robin Reagler
How Distant the City - Freesia McKee
Shopgirls - Marissa Higgins
Riddle - Diane Fortney
When She Woke She Was an Open Field - Hilary Brown
A Crown of Violets - Renée Vivien tr. Samantha Pious
Fireworks in the Graveyard - Joy Ladin
Social Dance - Carolyn Boll
The Force of Gratitude - Janice Gould
Spine - Sarah Caulfield
I Wore the Only Garden I've Ever Grown - Kathryn Leland
Diatribe from the Library - Farrell Greenwald Brenner

Blind Girl Grunt - Constance Merritt
Acid and Tender - Jen Rouse
Beautiful Machinery - Wendy DeGroat
Odd Mercy - Gail Thomas
The Great Scissor Hunt - Jessica K. Hylton
A Bracelet of Honeybees - Lynn Strongin
Whirlwind @ Lesbos - Risa Denenberg
The Body's Alphabet - Ann Tweedy
First name Barbie last name Doll - Maureen Bocka
Heaven to Me - Abe Louise Young
Sticky - Carter Steinmann
Tiger Laughs When You Push - Ruth Lehrer
Night Ringing - Laura Foley
Paper Cranes - Dinah Dietrich
On Loving a Saudi Girl - Carina Yun
The Burn Poems - Lynn Strongin
I Carry My Mother - Lesléa Newman
Distant Music - Joan Annsfire
The Awful Suicidal Swans - Flower Conroy
Joy Street - Laura Foley
Chiaroscuro Kisses - G.L. Morrison
The Lillian Trilogy - Mary Meriam
Lady of the Moon - Amy Lowell, Lillian Faderman, Mary Meriam
Irresistible Sonnets - ed. Mary Meriam
Lavender Review - ed. Mary Meriam

www.ingramcontent.com/pod-product-compliance
Lightning Source LLC
Chambersburg PA
CBHW060221050426
42446CB00013B/3133